I0465351

WILLS, TRUST, AND ESTATE ADMINISTRATION

This is a brief synopsis of wills, trust, and estate administration

Page formation is designed for notes . I hope this will familiarizes

You with the vocabulary of wills, trusts, and estate administration,

And briefly describes the purposes of wills and trust.

As mentioned above , pages are formatted for notes on the subject

Topic , this will aid you by keeping all notes in one collective place.

Best of luck to you !

Notes

(use this space to record notes)

(use this space to record notes)

(FOOT NOTES)

The purposes of wills and trust.......

NOTES:

(USE THIS SPACE FOR NOTES)

(USE THIS SPACE FOR IMPORTANT INFORMATION)

(ADD FOOT NOTES)

ESTATE PLANNING AND ADMINISTRATION INTRODUCES YOU.......

NOTES:

(USE THIS SPACE FOR NOTES)

(USE THIS SPACE FOR NOTES)

(FOOT NOTES)

DEMONSTRATING ITS IMPORTANCE TO INDIVIDUALS AND FAMILIES

NOTES:

(USE THIS SPACE FOR NOTES)

(FOOT NOTES)

DISCUSSING THE PROCESS AND INTRODUCING YOU TO PARTICIPANTS IN THE PROCESS......

NOTES:

(USE THIS SPACE FOR NOTES)

(USE THIS SPACE FOR FOOT NOTES)

PARTICPANTS AND THE PROPER COURTS………

NOTES:

(USE THIS SPACE FOR NOTES)

(USE THIS SPACE FOR NOTES)

(FOOT NOTES)

Describes in greater detail the participants......

NOTES:

(USE THIS SPACE FOR NOTES)

FOOT NOTES:

In probate proceedings........

NOTES:

(USE THIS SPACE TO RECORD NOTES)

(USE THIS SPACE TO RECORD IMPORTANT INFORMATION)

(FOOT NOTES)

THE FUNCTIONS OF THE PROBATE COURT....

NOTES:

(USE THIS SPACE FOR NOTES)

(USE THIS SPACE TO RECORD IMPORTANT INFORMATION)

(FOOT NOTES)

AND THE ASSISTANCE PROVIDED BY THE LAW.....

NOTES:

(USE THIS SPACE FOR NOTES)

(USE THIS SPACE FOR IMPORTANT INFORMATION)

BY THE LAW FIRM'S PARALEGAL.........

NOTES:

(USE THIS SPACE FOR NOTES)

(USE THIS SPACE TO RECORD IMPORTANT INFORMATION)

(FOOT NOTES)

TO THE PERSONAL REPRESENTATIVE.....

NOTES:

(USE THIS SPACE FOR NOTES)

(USE THIS SPACE TO RECORD IMPORTANT INFORMATION)

(FOOT NOTES)

OF THE DECEDENT'S ESTATE..........

NOTES:

(USE THIS SPACE FOR NOTES)

(USE THIS SPACE TO RECORD IMPORTANT INFORMATION)

FOOT NOTES:

PROPERTY.......

NOTES:

(USE THIS SPACE FOR NOTES)

(USE THIS SPACE TO RECORD IMPORTANT INFORMATION)

(FOOT NOTES)

CONCEPTS RELATED TO WILLS.....

NOTES:

(USE THIS SPACE TO RECORD NOTES)

(USE THIS SPACE TO RECORD IMPORTANT INFORMATION)

(FOOT NOTES

NOTES:

(USE THIS SPACE TO RECORD NOTES)

(USE THIS SPACE TO RECORD IMPORTANT INFORMATION)

(FOOT NOTES)

YOU WILL LEARN WHAT INTERESTS EXIST.....

NOTES:

(USE THIS SPACE TO RECORD NOTES)

(USE THIS SPACE TO RECORD IMPORTANT INFORMATION)

(FOOT NOTES)

IN PROPERTY AND SPECIAL CONCEPTS......

NOTES:

(USE THIS SPACE TO RECORD NOTES)

(USE THIS SPACE TO RECORD IMPORTANT INFORMATION)

ARE APPLICABLE IN MOST COMMUNITY PROPERTY STATES....

NOTES:

(USE THIS SPACE TO RECORD NOTES)

(USE THIS SPACE TO RECORD IMPORTANT INFORMATION)

(FOOT NOTES)

THE PURPOSE OF A WILL.......

NOTES:

(USE THIS SPACE TO RECORD NOTES)

(use this space to record important information)

FOOT NOTES:

INTRODUCES YOU TO LAWS OF SUCCESSION.......

NOTES:

(USE THIS SPACE TO RECORD NOTES)

(USE THIS SPACE TO RECORD IMPORTANT INFORMATION)

(FOOT NOTES)

THE CONSEQUENCES OF DEATH WITH.......

NOTES:

(USE THIS SPACE TO RECORD NOTES)

(USE THIS SPACE TO RECORD IMPORTANT INFORMATION)

OR WITHOUT A WILL..........

NOTES:

(USE THIS SPACE TO RECORD NOTES)

(USE THIS SPACE TO RECORD IMPORTANT INFORMATION)

FOOT NOTES;

AND THE CONCEPT OF INHERITANCE RIGHTS......

NOTES:

(USE THIS SPACE TO RECORD NOTES)

(USE THIS SPACE TO RECORD IMPORTANT INFORMATION)

(FOOT NOTES)

AND WILL SUBSTITUTES............

NOTES:

(USE THIS SPACE TO RECORD NOTES)

(USE THIS SPACE TO RECORD IMPORTANT INFORMATION)

(FOOT NOTES)

WILLS: VALIDITY REQUIREMENTS.........

NOTES:

(USE THIS SPACE TO RECORD NOTES)

(USE THIS SPACE TO RECORD IMPORTANT INFORMATION)

EXPLAINS THE COMPONENTS OF A VALID WILL.......

Notes:

(use this space to record notes)

(use this space to record important information)

(foot notes)

HOW A WILL IS CREATED , WHO MUST SIGN A WILL......

NOTES:

(USE THIS SPACE FOR NOTES)

(USE THIS SPACE TO RECORD IMPORTANT INFORMATION)

(FOOT NOTES)

HOW THE WILL MAY BE MODIFIED OR........

NOTES:

(USE THIS SPACE TO RECORD NOTES)

(FOOT NOTES)

REVOKED, AND WHO MAY CONTEST THE AUTHENTICITY....

NOTES:

(USE THIS SPACE TO RECORD NOTES)

(USE THIS SPACE TO RECORD IMPORTANT INFORMATION)

(FOOT NOTES)

PREPARING TO DRAFT A WILL........

NOTES:

(USE THIS SPACE TO RECORD NOTES)

(USE THIS SPACE TO RECORD IMPORTANT INFORMATION)

9FOOT NOTES)

WILL EXPLAIN HOW A PARALEGAL GATHERS THE INFORMATION....

NOTES:

(USE THIS SPACE TO RECORD NOTES)

(USE THIS SPACE TO RECORD IMPORTANT INFORMATION)

(FOOT NOTES)

FROM A CLIENT WHOSE WILL IS TO BE PREPARED.......

NOTES:

(USE THIS SPACE TO RECORD NOTES)

(USE THIS SPACE TO RECORD IMPORTANT INFORMATION)

(FOOT NOTES)

DRAFTING AND EXCUTING A WILL.....

NOTES:

(USE THIS SPACE TO RECORD NOTES)

(USE THIS SPACE TO RECORD IMPORTANT INFORMATION)

()FOOT NOTES)

EXPLAINS HOW THE CLIENT'S OBJECTIVES ARE MATCHED WITH...

NOTES:

(USE THIS SPACE TO RECORD NOTES)

(USE THIS SPACE FOR IMPORTANT INFORMATION)

WITH SPECIFIC CLAUSES IN THE WILL AND WHAT PRECAUTIONS....

NOTES:

(USE THIS SPACE TO RECORD NOTES)

(USE THIS SPACE TO RECORD IMPORTANT INFORMATION)

ARE TAKEN IN THE EXECUTION OF THE WILL.

NOTES:

(USE THIS SPACE TO RECORD NOTES)

(USE THIS SPACE TO RECORD IMPORTANT INFORMATION)

www.ingramcontent.com/pod-product-compliance
Lightning Source LLC
Chambersburg PA
CBHW060007230526
45472CB00008B/1987